W9-AET-790

DIGITAL AND INFORMATION LITERACY ™

UNDERSTANDING DIGITAL PIRACY

SUSAN MEYER

rosen publishing's
rosen
central®

New York

Published in 2014 by The Rosen Publishing Group, Inc.
29 East 21st Street, New York, NY 10010

Library of Congress Cataloging-in-Publication Data

Meyer, Susan, 1986-
Understanding digital piracy/Susan Meyer.—1st ed.—New York: Rosen, c2014
    p. cm.—(Digital and information literacy)
Includes bibliographical references and index.
ISBN: 978-1-4488-9514-4
1. Piracy (Copyright)–United States–Juvenile literature. 2. Peer-to-peer architecture (Computer networks)–Law and legislation–United States. 3. Copyright and electronic data processing–United States–Juvenile literature. 4. Piracy (Copyright)–United States.
I. Title.
KF3080 .M49 2014
346.7304'82

Manufactured in the United States of America

CPSIA Compliance Information: Batch #S13YA: For further information, contact Rosen Publishing, New York, New York, at 1-800-237-9932.

CONTENTS

INTRODUCTION

In times past, if you wanted to watch a movie, get new software for your computer, or listen to a band's new CD, you had to either go to the store and pay for it or borrow it from a friend. Today, the Internet has changed the speed and methods with which we gain and use media content, including music, books, television shows, and movies. As the Internet has evolved, it has become a source of both information and entertainment around the globe. No longer do we have to go to the store, movie theater, or cable company to buy entertainment. It can now be downloaded directly from the Internet. There are a number of sites that legally sell content like books, movies, and music for people to purchase. However, there are also a number of sites where people can download and stream this content for free.

For free? That sounds better than paying for the same content, you might think. Unfortunately, many of these free sites are also illegal. When you download a television show, movie, CD, or book from an illegal site, you are stealing, plain and simple. It is the same as if you went into a store, grabbed a DVD off the shelf, and ran off without paying for it. Interestingly, many people who would never consider shoplifting are perfectly fine with stealing content from the Internet. Downloading copyrighted content from the Internet without permission is an act called digital piracy. There are more than 146 million visits a day to Web sites that engage in digital piracy.

Sharing music with friends can be a fun way to learn about new bands. Just make sure you are sharing your music in a legal way and with real friends—not strangers.

More shocking, statistics show that 70 percent of Internet users don't believe Internet piracy is wrong.

Unlike when shoplifting in a brick-and-mortar store, the criminal cannot see some of the people who will suffer for his or her crime, such as the store owner and employees. Even though the Internet puts a distance between the anonymous criminal and his or her unseen victim, people are still hurt by acts of digital piracy. Over $12.5 billion is lost each year in the music industry alone due to online piracy. This doesn't affect only the wealthy heads of industry or even the artists you like well enough to want to listen to their music. This affects everyone in the industry. Overall, it amounts to more than seventy-one thousand jobs lost in the United States each year.

The issue of digital piracy has become a debate between consumers who believe Internet-based content should be free and accessible and content creators and providers who believe they should be fairly compensated for the work that they do. The bottom line is that, if everyone plays by the rules, consumers can pay a fair and reasonable price for their entertainment. At the same time, artists and providers can and should receive fair and reasonable compensation for their hard work.

⊙ **Chapter 1**

The Evolution of Digital Piracy

Technological advancements and the spread of the Internet have rapidly changed the way that content is obtained, transferred, and consumed. Digital and Internet technology has allowed people all around the world to download large multimedia files at very fast rates. Along the way, the idea of sharing files and passing them from friend to friend, or even uploading them for strangers to view and use, has also become commonplace.

What Is Digital Piracy?

Digital piracy is the illegal copying and distribution of copyrighted content via electronic means. Streaming a video from an illegal site or downloading a file without paying for it qualifies as digital piracy. Anyone who sells digital assets online is at risk of losing money to Internet piracy. Digital assets include everything from TV shows and movies to games, software, e-books, and music—any content that can be distributed over the Internet. Digital piracy causes billions of dollars in losses each year throughout many different industries.

Downloading music or movies onto CDs or DVDs is not the same as buying CDs or DVDs. Unless you pay to download content from a legal site, it is digital piracy.

When defining what digital piracy means, it's important to understand that things you may do every day are actually considered illegal—it is theft punishable by law. If you buy a print book, CD, or DVD, it's not a problem to loan it to friends to enjoy. So why is it a problem to share media that you have purchased on the Internet? The difference is that while you might loan a movie or CD to friends to watch or listen to, until relatively recently you would not have expected them to make a copy of the content either physically (by burning a CD) or digitally (by downloading a copy on their computer). If, after friends borrowed the content, they wanted a copy of their own, they would have had to purchase it.

Today, however, with the ability to "rip" CDs and copy and download other kinds of digital content, your friends could possess an infinite amount of content that they haven't paid a dime for. Burning a copy of a CD, rather than paying for a copy or downloading the MP3 from a legitimate music site, takes money out of the pockets of hardworking men and women. It means that the musicians, producers, employees of the record label, and everyone else who contributed to making the CDs content, would lose the money that they deserved for their work.

Oversharing with the Help of P2P Networks

Before home computers with Internet access were common, digital piracy didn't exist. People could still make illegal copies of copyrighted materials, but they couldn't share them instantly with billions of people, across a worldwide network, at the click of a button. The most common type of digital piracy is the usage of online, peer-to-peer networks, otherwise known as P2P networks. A P2P network is a place where people can upload their copies of movies, music, reports, software, and other digital files so that other people around the world can download them to their computers and digital devices.

The first major P2P file-sharing network was Napster. Napster was started in 1998 by a Northeastern University student named Shawn Fanning. Fanning was only eighteen at the time he created Napster in his dorm room, along with his brother John and his friend Shawn Parker. Shawn Fanning noticed that MP3s, a popular file format for music, were being uploaded to the Internet in increasing numbers. Yet he also realized that there wasn't an easy way for people to find this uploaded music that they could then download to their personal computers and digital devices. His idea was to create a site where the music was well organized and people could share their music with a large community of online users. The way a P2P network works is that when you want to download a song using a

Napster was one of the earliest file-sharing services. People would illegally share music on the site and then burn downloaded music onto CDs, using devices like the one seen here.

program like Napster, you are actually downloading it not from Napster itself but directly from another user's computer. That person could be your next-door neighbor or a stranger living halfway around the world.

Napster took off in a big way. Suddenly, thousands of people were making copies of copyrighted songs and uploading them to the Internet. Artists and record companies were upset that the people who used to pay for the content they spent time and money producing were now getting it for free. Napster was particularly popular among college students, even after 40 percent of U.S. college and universities banned the program. Napster eventually ceased operations due to legal issues surrounding copyright infringement. It was later relaunched as a legal site where users pay to download music.

File sharing and digital piracy did not end with Napster, however. Soon, new sites were springing up, including Freenet and Gnutella in 2000. Freenet was a type of P2P network called a darknet. A darknet is a file-sharing network in which connections are made between peers anonymously. Because the users' IP addresses and other identifying information are not shared, it makes it harder for the government and law enforcement to identify and prosecute them.

Gnutella was a P2P network similar to Napster, except for one crucial difference: unlike Napster, which had a centralized system from which all downloads and uploads were made, Gnutella was decentralized. This meant that it was much

Sharing music on the Internet

Gnutella is one of the new file-sharing programs that makes it harder to trace downloaded material because, unlike Napster, it doesn't use a central database.

HOW GNUTELLA WORKS

1. A user asks whether a file on the network exists

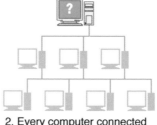

2. Every computer connected responds either "yes" or "no"

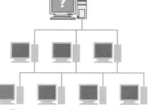

3. The user's computer then connects directly to the computer to download the file

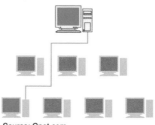

HOW NAPSTER WORKS

1. Napster users log on, adding their music catalogs to a master database

2. The user initiates a song search

3. Napster database says, "Computer A has a song"

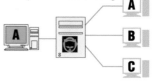

4. The user downloads the song directly from Computer A

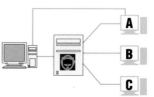

Source: Cnet.com
The Dallas Morning News

© 2013 MCT

This infographic illustrates the differences between the file-sharing services Gnutella and Napster and how users connected to and downloaded content from each.

harder to shut down. The Gnutella software, named for the GNU General Public License for open-source software, was openly shared so that anyone could use it. This led to many more file-sharing networks using Gnutella, including the popular Limewire and Morpheus networks. Compared to Napster, these newer networks operated at higher speeds. Also, since all the copyrighted material was stored on users' computers and not in one central directory, the sites were able to dodge many legal actions.

The Perils and Promise of BitTorrent

In 2001, a programmer named Bram Cohen designed BitTorrent, a new way to share content online. BitTorrent provided a way to exchange large

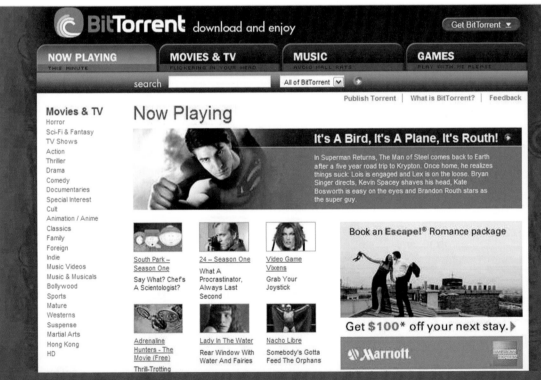

This screenshot shows the BitTorrent Web site. This is a legal Web site launched by the company to sell downloads of movies and music licensed from the studios.

files and information over the Internet. Instead of uploading a file from one user as with traditional P2P networks, on BitTorrent the information is broken up into parts. These different parts are then downloaded from a swarm of hosts. As each user receives a new piece of the file, he or she becomes a source of that piece of data for others. This relieves the original owner of the file from having to send that piece to every computer or user who wants a copy. It also makes it far harder to identify the individuals responsible for uploading and downloading copyrighted content.

While the BitTorrent system has been used to facilitate illegal sites like TorrentSpy and the Pirate Bay, it has also many legal uses as well. BitTorrent has received licenses from a number of Hollywood studios to distribute their content legally. The popular social networking Web site Facebook also uses BitTorrent to make updates available to its users. Even many universities and the government of the United Kingdom have used BitTorrent to distribute information.

With all of these digital piracy options available for Internet users to exploit, those trying to protect their copyrighted content have a big battle to fight. But major industries are fighting back against both Internet sites that facilitate illegal downloads and the would-be pirates who illegally download and consume copyrighted material.

Chapter 2

Fighting Back Against Piracy

As new technologies have emerged to make it easier for people to illegally download and share music, movies, books, and other digital content, so, too, have the creators of this content risen up to vigilantly protect their work. Across the music, movie, television, and publishing industries, players both major and minor have begun to aggressively protect their copyrights, their best interests, and their hard-earned income and earnings.

The MPAA and the Movie Industry

A major player in the fight against digital piracy is the Motion Picture Association of America (MPAA). The MPAA is an organization made up of the six biggest Hollywood studios. It has faced both support and criticism for its attempts to combat the online piracy of movies. Its first attempt to halt illegal downloads and copyright infringement involved a series of ad campaigns designed to reach out to the everyday people who

When Pirate Bay was shut down by the Swedish government for acts of digital piracy, hundreds of protesters took to the streets of Stockholm to support Pirate Bay's actions.

didn't see anything wrong with downloading a movie here or there. "You wouldn't steal a car," one ad pointed out. "Don't steal a movie."

In response to continued illegal downloading of copyright-protected movies, the MPAA began to take legal action against the illegal downloaders and the sites that hosted them. In the early and mid-2000s, the MPAA took legal action against a number of peer-to-peer file-sharing sites. Two of the most well-known examples were the sites Razorback and the Pirate Bay. The Pirate Bay was a Swedish site for BitTorrent sharing. In 2006, Swedish police were able to shut down the site for three days. However, the publicity resulting from the raid inspired even more people

File   Edit   View   Favorites   Tools   Help

COPYRIGHT INFRINGEMENT GOES TO COLLEGE

Copyright Infringement Goes to College

One place where digital piracy is particularly common is on college campuses. This isn't surprising. College students often don't have a lot of money, and they are also usually fans of the latest movies and music. In an anonymous study by the Recording Industry Association of America (RIAA), 56 percent of full-time students reported illegally downloading music regularly. Both the RIAA and the MPAA have fined college students for their practices. They have also urged college officials to take action in discouraging their students from breaking copyright law.

Many colleges now include guidelines for legal and proper Internet and downloading practices during student orientation. At some schools, students can actually receive administrative punishment even if they aren't sued or fined by the RIAA or the MPAA. At Michigan State University, the first time a student is caught illegally downloading content, he or she is given a warning. Second-time offenders must watch an eight-minute video on digital piracy created by the RIAA. A third offense means the student can be suspended for up to a semester.

to join the site. Overall, many people considered the Pirate Bay raid to be a misstep by the MPAA that worsened the situation.

The RIAA and the Music Industry

The Recording Industry Association of American is an organization that represents the music industry in the United States. It is made up of

The Recording Industry Association of America took legal action against the peer-to-peer file-sharing site Kazaa for helping enable users to commit copyright infringement.

members from different record labels and distributors. One of its stated goals is to protect intellectual property rights. These are the rights that give artists control over the works they produce, such as music. It is not surprising that the RIAA opposes the illegal downloading of its music. Illegal downloads account for a loss of billions of dollars for the industry each year. According to a 2010 *New York Times* article, the industry

17

believes that 95 percent of the music downloaded worldwide is acquired illegally.

Like the MPAA, the RIAA tries to combat illegal downloading by suing individual lawbreakers and the P2P networks that facilitate them. To identify lawbreakers, the RIAA traces the IP address of the person downloading and sharing music. Usually, it makes an offer to settle the matter out of court if the guilty party agrees to pay a fine. These settlement fines can be as much as $750 for each copyrighted work—such as a single song—that is illegally downloaded

In 2000, the heavy metal band Metallica sued the file-sharing site Napster when one of its songs appeared on the site before it was even officially released and put on sale. The RIAA supported Metallica and filed suit against Napster. A judge ruled that the file-sharing network needed to take steps to prevent the trading of copyrighted music on its network. Napster could not comply with the ruling without essentially putting itself out of business as a free site, and it did indeed shut down in 2001.

After settling the lawsuit by paying $26 million to music creators and copyright owners, Napster attempted to relaunch as a subscription service. Its former users were uninterested in paying for a service they once received for free, and Napster lost most of its customers. It has since been bought and sold by numerous companies and, in 2011, merged with the subscription-based music streaming service Rhapsody.

In 2006, the RIAA won a settlement from Kazaa, one of many P2P networks similar to Napster. This meant that Kazaa had to pay record companies over $100 million. It would also have to take steps to restrict its use for the illegal downloading of copyrighted materials and transition into a paid music site. Kazaa now operates as a music subscription service that allows users to download an unlimited number of songs for a monthly fee. In 2010, the RIAA also won a similar settlement against the P2P network Limewire.

The problem is that for all the individuals and network owners who are caught and fined or shut down for their role in illegal downloads of copyrighted material, there are still millions of illegal downloaders out there. And new networks pop up every day to facilitate their pirating efforts. Even if the music industry wins its lawsuits and receives hefty settlements, it is still losing millions of dollars in legitimate sales and spiraling court costs and legal fees. For this reason, the music industry has waged war against digital piracy in court. It has also had to adapt its way of doing business to the changing digital atmosphere.

Digital Rights Management

As technology has evolved that makes it easier to share data, the movie, television, and music industries have

DVDs, Blu-ray discs, and digital copies of popular blockbusters such as this one often have technologies that prevent the purchasers from sharing the content with too many people.

devised a few technological tricks of their own. They have developed methods to prevent people from spreading digital content illegally. This is called digital rights management, or DRM. Any type of technology that is used to prevent the practice of piracy is considered DRM. An example of DRM is a movie studio releasing a DVD with coding that limits the number of times the disc can be copied to two. Another example might be a music studio releasing a CD that includes technology that jams ripping software, making it impossible to be copied at all.

MYTHS & FACTS

MYTH Downloading music, movies, books, software, and games from the Internet is anonymous.

FACT Copyright infringement is a crime, and those who hold the copyright can track who downloaded the content by his or her IP address. This is the address for your computer. Like your home address, it is unique to you and can be traced to where you live.

MYTH It's OK to illegally download music, movies, books, software, and games online as long as you don't do it very much and don't share what you download.

FACT While the law originally went after only major offenders of copyright infringement, there is no minimum for the amount of downloads before you can be sued. Some college students have had complaints brought against them for downloading just a single file. Additionally, stealing is stealing no matter how little or much you do it.

MYTH Downloading music doesn't hurt sales.

FACT The belief that people who download or stream music for free wouldn't have paid for them anyway has been proven false by the amount of money lost by the movie, television, and music industries since the rise of digital piracy. Online piracy has cut into national music sales by nearly a third since 1999. These losses affect every-one, from the record store clerks, songwriters, and technicians to the artists themselves. Online piracy also hurts the development of new music, films, artists, and talent.

Chapter 3

Laying Down the Law

As technology has evolved, so, too, has copyright law. Copyright is a protection granted in the U.S. Constitution to give ownership of a work to its creator. In the 1990s, lawmakers began changing the existing copyright law so that it included copies made and shared over the Internet.

In 1998, Congress passed the Digital Millennium Copyright Act (DMCA). The act was intended to meet the growing needs of the digital age. It created harsher penalties for people who practiced copyright infringement on the Internet. It was a way to help enforce the laws of the World Intellectual Property Organization (WIPO). WIPO is an organization created in 1996 to deal with the changing nature of copyright issues in the digital age.

Caught in the NET?

The DMCA isn't the only law created by the government to fight against copyright infringement. The No Electronic Theft Act (NET) was passed

WIPO | OMPI
WORLD
INTELLECTUAL PROPERTY
ORGANIZATION

The singer and songwriter Stevie Wonder lends his support to the Assemblies of the World Intellectual Property Organization. Many recording artists have begun to speak out about having their content stolen by fans.

in 1997. It made it possible to prosecute people who practiced copyright infringement even if they didn't plan to benefit financially from the act. So people who simply share songs or movies with friends and are not attempting to re-sell the product or charge someone else for its use could still end up in big trouble. They could be fined up to $250,000 or even spend up to five years in jail.

NET addressed one of the new issues of copyright infringement in the digital age by targeting the average user rather than the major, profit-motivated content thieves. Many people who committed the act weren't trying to make money from it. They were just trying to access and share content without paying for it. But these were the ordinary people who were costing the media industries millions and millions of dollars in lost sales.

File   Edit   View   Favorites   Tools   Help

     DIGITAL PIRACY AROUND THE WORLD

Digital Piracy Around the World

Digital piracy isn't just a problem in the United States (although Americans are the greatest offenders) but worldwide as well. In recent years, Americans have been responsible for nearly one hundred million illegal music downloads annually. The second biggest offender with about forty-three million illegal music downloads is the United Kingdom, with Italy, Canada, and Brazil rounding out the top five.

Copyright laws are not universal. Each country has its own unique laws pertaining to copyright. Downloading copied music is legal in Canada as long as it isn't resold or otherwise distributed. However, the Copyright Modernization Act, passed in Canada in 2012 and going into effect fully in 2013, may begin limiting what people can upload to file-sharing networks. The Netherlands, Spain, and Panama have similar views on digital copyright law.

Free Content for All

While many laws and practices have been put in place to prevent or discourage the sharing of copyrighted digital content, there are some organizations that take the opposite view. They believe that all Internet-based content should be free and that everyone can benefit from the ability to share content at a rapid rate. These usually nonprofit organizations work to make as much content as possible available to everyone.

This is not to say that they work against copyright law or undermine the artists and creators of content who choose to copyright their work. The

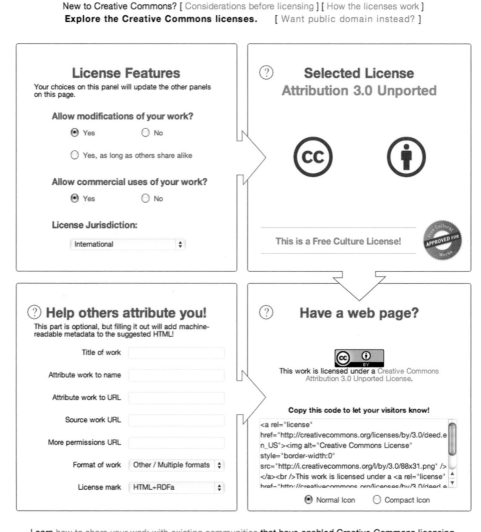

You can learn how to share your work with communities that use the Creative Commons license. Just visit the Creative Commons Web site (http://creativecommons.org) and follow the simple steps that are also outlined above.

nonprofit Creative Commons provides legal tools and licenses for people who want to share their work with others. It allows the artists themselves to define who can use their work and how. These copyright licenses work alongside existing copyright law to suit the needs of the content creator. This means that not only is more content free and open for use online, but also that it is up to the content creator to decide how or if its use will be restricted.

Another example of a nonprofit organization supporting free Internet-based content is the Free Software Foundation (FSF). This foundation believes that computer programs and software should be shared by and available to all users for free. By making such content readily available to all, the FSF believes that more people will be able to collaborate on improving the content. This, in turn, will enable new innovations and an ongoing spur to technological advances that will benefit one and all.

Chapter 4

The Future of Digital Content

New copyright protection laws have been put in place, and affected industries have been launching aggressive efforts to stem the tide of digital piracy and illegal downloading. Yet the ready access to content that technology now provides has also forced content providers to accept some hard realities and confront the practicalities of the brave new digital world. Some of the most aggressive proposed anti-piracy legislation has failed to pass after igniting firestorms of popular displeasure. Meanwhile, the technology that makes digital piracy possible continues to advance by leaps and bounds.

The Failure of Anti-Piracy Legislation

When the MPAA and RIAA tried to flex their muscles in support of anti-piracy legislation, they failed—badly. Congress considered enacting the Stop Online Piracy Act (SOPA) in 2011–2012. SOPA provided for harsher penalties against sites that enabled digital piracy. It would allow for the issuing of court orders that would deter advertisers from working with Web sites that

Internet users hold a protest in Dublin, Ireland, against the Stop Internet Piracy Act. There was a huge backlash against SOPA, both in worldwide street protests and in online demonstrations.

supported copyright infringement. It would also have kept search engines from linking to these Web sites. Because most people use search engines to find Web content, this would mean Web sites containing and/or offering content that infringed on copyright laws would basically disappear from the Internet. In addition, the law would have updated existing criminal laws to make illegal not only the downloading of content from illegal sites but also the mere streaming of unauthorized content.

SOPA led to a widespread Internet backlash. The opponents of the act thought it would negatively impact free speech and the availability of content on the Internet. Ultimately, SOPA, like the Fair Use Act, did not pass.

File   Edit   View   Favorites   Tools   Help

 A HISTORY MAKING PROTEST

A History-Making Protest

The Stop Online Piracy Act was very controversial because, while it was intended to help limit piracy over the Internet, opponents worried that it would also limit free speech. Several popular Web sites, including the American version of the free encyclopedia Wikipedia and the popular message board site Reddit, shut down their sites in protest on January 18, 2012. Instead of their usual content, the sites were replaced with banners explaining their opposition. Other major Web sites that chose to participate in the January 18 blackout included the Oatmeal, the Web comic XKCD, Boing Boing, and Major League Gamer.

WIKIPEDIA

Imagine a World
Without Free Knowledge

For over a decade, we have spent millions of hours building the largest encyclopedia in human history. Right now, the U.S. Congress is considering legislation that could fatally damage the free and open Internet. For 24 hours, to raise awareness, we are blacking out Wikipedia. Learn more.

Contact your representatives.

Your ZIP code: [   ] Look up

For twenty-four hours on January 18, 2012, the free, crowd-sourced online encyclopedia, Wikipedia, showed this page instead of its regular content in protest of SOPA.

The protestors made the point that, under the proposed law, all Web sites that support user content would be responsible for what their users did with it. This would be unfair, unreasonable, and impractical, they reasoned. It would be akin to a library being held responsible for the ways in which its patrons used the information they encountered there. This wouldn't just affect online communities like Reddit and Wikipedia but also social networks like YouTube, Twitter, and Flickr. The January 18 protest was considered the largest organized online protest in history.

Technology on Both Sides of the Battle

Digital piracy is incredibly common now, but researchers believe it will become an even larger issue in the future. According to a 2012 survey by the Business Software Alliance, 57 percent of computer users pirate software. A survey conducted by the market research company Interpret found that 36 percent of its sixty million respondents admitted to illegally downloading music in just the last three months. These numbers are only set to increase as technologies like smartphones and tablets make it that much easier to download desired content on the go.

The technology used by pirates is continuously improving and adapting to the latest conditions, laws, and anti-piracy efforts. The BitTorrent site Pirate

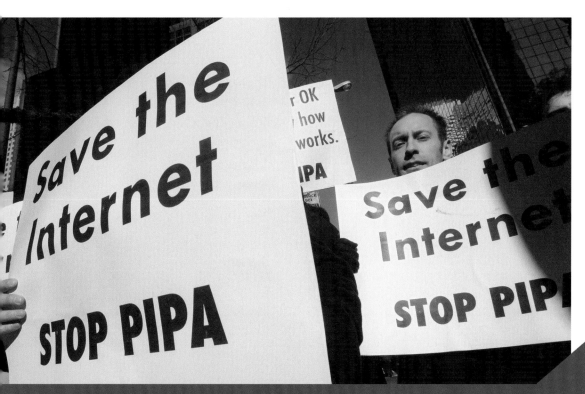

Many people committed to an open and free Internet strongly opposed the Stop Internet Piracy Act (SOPA) and the Protect IP Act (PIPA). Above, technology activists who believed the bills would encourage censorship protested outside two senators' offices in New York City.

Bay was briefly shut down for supporting copyright infringement on its servers. In response, the Web site took its code and offered it to users as a free downloadable file. This meant that anyone could copy the code and install it on his or her own server. Suddenly, there were millions of smaller versions of Pirate Bay operating on personal computers worldwide. Despite the best efforts of the music, movie, television, publishing, and software industries, the pirates often seem to remain one step ahead. In March 2012, for example, a member of Pirate Bay announced that the site hoped to build floating drones. The drones would let people download content through wireless transmitters.

However, those fighting against digital piracy are also always at work creating new technology that will protect copyrighted material. Two brothers in Russia have formed a company called Pirate Pay. In 2009, they began creating a prototype for a file-sharing management system that prevents file sharing in P2P torrent networks. It prevents people from downloading files by garbling the IP address from which the file was uploaded. Without this information, a successful download cannot take place. While the brothers are still fine-tuning the technology, Pirate Pay has reported the successful prevention of around fifty thousand illegal downloads. It might seem like a minor accomplishment in the face of the millions of files downloaded illegally every day, but it's a small step in the right direction.

Chapter 5

Don't Be a Pirate

When you download or stream a copyright-protected movie, television show, video game, book, or song without paying for it, you are stealing. It's important to remember from whom you are stealing. The artists you love and respect are personally hurt by copyright theft.

When musicians speak about illegal downloading and the theft of their music, for example, they express not just a concern over the loss of money but also a sense of personal betrayal. The country music band the Dixie Chicks have this to say about digital piracy: "It may seem innocent enough, but every time you illegally download music, a songwriter doesn't get paid. And every time you swap that music with your friends, a new artist doesn't get a chance. Respect the artists you love by not stealing their music" (as quoted by Music United, an alliance of music industry organizations advocating against the illegal distribution of copyrighted music). Another recording artist, Sean "P Diddy" Combs, who is also a successful music producer, asks digital pirates to put themselves in the shoes of the musicians

Sean "P Diddy" Combs has spoken out against digital piracy. He, like many recording artists and record producers, believes it is wrong for the fans of his music to steal content after all the hard work he puts into it.

they affect: "Every day we're out pouring our heart and soul into making music for everyone to enjoy. What if you didn't get paid for your job?" (as quoted by Music United).

It isn't only the artists themselves who are hurt. Everyone who works in the music, movie, publishing, gaming, and other digital content industries are affected by the money and jobs lost due to illegal downloading. This includes everyone from the highest-paid executives to entry-level sound and computer technicians.

Getting Caught and Paying the Price

Beyond the ethical reasons to avoid piracy, there are a number of legal and financial consequences you can incur if you choose to download content illegally. Piracy is a crime, and people are increasingly being prosecuted in copyright cases. With so many people downloading illegal content every day, it's easy to feel like you can hide within the crowd and not get caught.

Skyler, a seventeen-year-old from New Mexico, thought he was safe from copyright fines because so many of his friends did it without even thinking about it. However, all of that changed when he downloaded the film *Hurt Locker* from a BitTorrent site. Authorities traced the download to his father's IP address and offered him a settlement for $2,900. Skyler's father is making him pay all of the money he owes. Skyler now must live with a huge debt and even bigger regrets. "Ever since this came about," he said, "I keep thinking to myself, 'Why didn't I just go to a Redbox and rent the movie, legally, for, you know, a dollar?'" (as quoted by Cambio.com). Sklyer is not alone. Many teens learn the hard way that assuming they won't get caught for illegal downloading can be a costly mistake.

In addition to the legal and moral arguments against digital piracy, consider that the Web sites that provide illegal downloads or streamed movies can often give your computer nasty viruses or spyware. These viruses and malware can slow down your machine. They can also spread to the computers of your friends, parents, teachers, and others you communicate with via e-mail. In some cases, viruses or spyware might also steal valuable personal information that is stored on your computer, such as credit card, bank account, and Social Security numbers. When it comes to illegally downloading music, movies, books, and games, the risks just aren't worth the reward.

Legal and Responsible Downloading Options

Just because you want to avoid pirating digital content from the Internet doesn't mean you can't still enjoy the ease and affordability of downloading your favorite music, movies, and games in the blink of an eye. All the media industries affected by piracy allow for legal ways to take advantage of

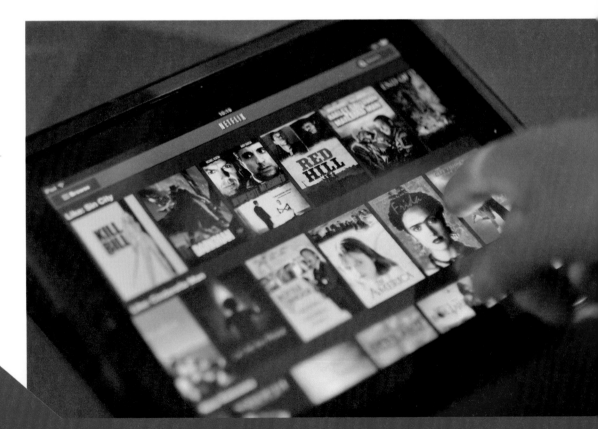

Sites like Netflix are a great place to stream movies and television shows legally for a low monthly cost. Best of all, movies rented from Netflix can be streamed on computers or mobile devices, or, with the right connectors, even displayed on a television.

digital distribution of their content. After all, who wants to go to a video store to rent the latest flick when you can simply download it to your computer in the time it takes the popcorn to pop? And what if you don't want to buy a whole CD but just one song? Not only are there plenty of options online for getting the latest content without leaving the comfort of your home, they are also cost effective and perfectly legal.

Cable providers and sites like iTunes allow you to buy or rent movies that will download directly onto your computer, smartphone, or tablet. If you buy the movie, it's yours to keep and enjoy. If you rent it, the file will expire after a period of time (usually twenty-four hours). There are also sites where you can enjoy movies or television shows without downloading them at all. These movies stream on your computer, which means you will need Internet access the entire time you are watching them. Popular sites include Netflix, which was originally a video service that sent DVDs through the mail, but now includes a sizable collection of movies that stream online. To access the Netflix collection of movies, you must pay a monthly subscription. Hulu.com is another source for television shows and some movies. The site shows some free content that is legal and properly licensed by the television networks, but you can view premium shows and movies if you pay a monthly fee.

There are some places where you can legally watch movies online without paying for them. Sites like OpenCulture.com and Archive.org host streaming movies that are in the public domain. This means that the copyright has expired for these films, and they can legally be shown without infringement. OpenCulture has around five hundred classic films available, and Archive.org, which is organized by the Internet Archive Project, has a much larger collection of public domain films. Of course, you won't find any new releases on these sites. But that doesn't mean they don't have a wide range of films across all genres, from horror and sci-fi to romance and comedy.

For listening to music, there are a number of sites like iTunes and Amazon.com where you can buy entire albums or just a track or two. Amazon and iTunes both offer a selection of free songs. These are mostly songs by

There are many legal options for listening to music online. Most allow you to stream or download music not only to a computer but also to tablets, smartphones, or other mobile listening devices.

newer artists trying to get more exposure. Amazon offers over three thousand free songs for download. There are also monthly subscription sites like Rhapsody. These require users to pay a monthly subscription fee to access their enormous music collections (Rhapsody has over sixteen million songs).

Another option for listening to music online is through Internet radio sites like Pandora and Last.fm. These sites have a free option and a subscription option. Paying for the subscription allows you to listen to music with few or no commercial interruptions. You choose songs and artists you like and make

With so many options for downloading legal content to watch, listen to, and enjoy, there is no reason to do the wrong thing. Digital piracy is theft, and you run the risk of steep fines, real jail time, and a criminal record.

customized radio stations. These sites can help you find new music you might like based on your preferences. Like radio stations, you can listen to the songs only as they play (no rewinding or re-listening), and recording the songs for personal use later goes against the sites' terms of use.

Another site that offers free music for download is Jamendo, which has over 350,000 songs in its catalogue. Jamendo is able to offer free music legally because the artists who post the music to it release their work under Creative Commons licenses. This means they agree to allow their music to be not only downloaded and listened to for free but also to be modified by users.

For gamers, there are a number of places where you can play games online for free, like Pogo.com or Gamehouse.com. However, you may want to download games so that you have them to play even without Internet access. Many sites that offer free downloadable games will have the game work only for a limited time or with limited features and levels. After the trial period expires, the user must pay for the game. He or she will then receive the full, deluxe version.

As with movies and music, there are some Web sites that offer monthly subscriptions so that users can download all the games they want for one fee. Shockwave.com has a "Shockwave Unlimited" option in which users can play as many of the site's 1,300 games as they wish for one fee. Gamers can also pay for and download games directly onto their computers or game systems from game sites like the Wii Shop Channel (for the Nintendo Wii) or PlayStation.com (for all of the PlayStation systems). These sites often offer free demos of their games.

With so many options for the legal downloading of digital content at low—and sometimes even no—cost, there is no reason to consider digital piracy. The problem is many people just don't realize the consequences of their actions. On behalf of the creative artists you love, the industries that are a huge part of the economy, and the financial well-being of your friends and family, it's important that you make smart and responsible choices about where and how you obtain the digital content that you enjoy.

TEN GREAT QUESTIONS

TO ASK A DIGITAL LIBRARIAN OR COMPUTER SCIENCE TEACHER

1 What types of content can a copyright cover?

2 How can I tell if a site is offering illegal content to download?

3 Am I responsible for content I download if I didn't know that it was illegal?

4 Where can I find legal sites for downloading music/movies/books/games?

5 Can I use a copyrighted song in a video I post online?

6 Can I post a link to a copyrighted video or song on my blog or social network site?

7 Is it OK to share a music or movie file with my friends?

8 What are some laws that protect copyright holders from digital piracy?

9 If I publish my own work online, is it automatically copyrighted?

10 What are some ways I can help stop copyright infringement?

GLOSSARY

BitTorrent A method of sharing large files over the Internet by breaking them into pieces and having multiple hosts acquire and store pieces of the file.

compensation The money given to someone in payment for his or her work.

copyright infringement A violation of the exclusive legal ownership given to the creator of a product, work of art, intellectual property, or other kind of creative content.

Creative Commons license A flexible range of protections and freedoms that artists can choose to apply to their work to make it more accessible to users. The licensing tools give everyone from individual creators to large companies and institutions a simple, standardized way to grant copyright permissions to their creative work. The tools and their users form a growing digital commons, a pool of content that can be copied, distributed, edited, remixed, and built upon, all within the boundaries of copyright law.

darknet A P2P network with restricted access.

digital asset Something that is sold and distributed over the Internet; it can include e-books, movies, games, television shows, and music.

digital piracy The illegal copying and distribution of copyrighted content via electronic means.

DRM Digital rights management; any technology that helps protect digital property from illegal copying, theft, and distribution.

exploit To receive the benefit of something, often illegally and usually at someone else's expense.

intellectual property rights Protections that grant exclusive control of an idea or content (including discoveries, inventions, phrases, symbols, designs, and musical, literary, and artistic works) and how it will be used to its creator.

MPAA The Motion Picture Association of America; an organization made up of representatives from the six largest Hollywood studios.

open source Computer software in which the code is free and available for anyone to use and modify.

prototype An early working model of a new invention.

P2P networks Peer-to-peer networks; sites where people upload digital content so that others can download and use it.

public domain Content for which the copyright has expired or content that was never copyrighted.

RIAA The recording Industry Association of America; an organization made up of members of the recording industry to protect their business interests.

streaming The flowing of multimedia content that is constantly received by and presented to an end-user while being delivered by a provider. Content that is streamed on the Internet can't be downloaded and saved to a computer.

FOR MORE INFORMATION

Canadian Intellectual Property Office (CIPO)
Place du Portage I
50 Victoria Street, Room C-229
Gatineau, QC K1A 0C9
Canada
(866) 997-1936
Web site: http://www.cipo.ic.gc.ca
The CIPO is a government organization in Canada responsible for the
administration and processing of Canada's patents, trademarks,
copyrights, and industrial designs.

Canadian Internet Project (CIP)
Ryerson University School of Radio and Television Arts
Toronto, ON M5B 2K3
Canada
(416) 979-5000, ext.7549
Web site: http://www.ciponline.ca
The CIP is a Ryerson University–based, long-running research project
centering on Internet usage, trends, attitudes, and many other
factors in our relationship with the Web.

Creative Commons
444 Castro Street, Suite 900
Mountain View, CA 94041
(650) 294-4732
Web site: http://creativecommons.org
Creative Commons is a nonprofit organization that offers legal
tools, such as free licenses, to those who want to control how
their work is copyrighted. Its mission is to develop and support

licensing that maximizes digital creativity, sharing, and innovation.

Free Software Foundation (FSF)
51 Franklin Street, 5th Floor
Boston, MA 02110-1301
(617) 542-5942
Web site: http://www.fsf.org
The FSF is a nonprofit organization working to secure and provide free software for everyone. It manages the GNU project, which supports open-source software. It also leads campaigns against digital rights management (DRM) and software patents.

Internet Keep Safe Coalition
1401 K Street NW, Suite 600
Washington, DC 20005
(866) 794-7233
Web site: http://www.ikeepsafe.org
The Internet Keep Safe Coalition is an educational resource for children and families that educates about Internet safety and the ethics associated with Internet technologies.

Motion Picture Association of America (MPAA)
1600 Eye Street NW
Washington, DC 20006
(202) 293-1966
Web site: http://www.mpaa.org
The MPAA protects the interests of the motion picture, home video, and television industries in the United States and around the world.

Recording Industry Association of America (RIAA)
1025 F Street NW, 10th Floor
Washington, DC 20004
(202) 775-0101
Web site: http://www.riaa.com
The RIAA is the trade organization that supports the interests of the
    recording industry.

U.S. Copyright Office
101 Independence Avenue SE
Washington, DC 20559-6000
(202) 707-3000
Web site: http://www.copyright.gov
The Copyright Office is a division of the federal government that files
    copyright applications and provides answers to the questions of the
    general public regarding copyright law. It also offers expert advice
    on copyright policy and intellectual property protections to Congress,
    federal agencies, and the courts.

Web Sites

Due to the changing nature of Internet links, Rosen Publishing has developed
an online list of Web sites related to the subject of this book. This site is
updated regularly. Please use this link to access the list:

http://www.rosenlinks.com/DIL/Pirate

FOR FURTHER READING

Aufderheide, Patricia. *Reclaiming Fair Use: How to Put Balance Back in Copyright*. Chicago, IL: University of Chicago Press, 2011.

Curley, Robert, ed. *Issues in Cyberspace: From Privacy to Piracy*. New York, NY: Britannica Educational Publishing, 2012.

Doctorow, Cory. *Pirate Cinema*. New York, NY: Macmillian, 2012.

Espejo, Roman. *Copyright Infringement* (Opposing Viewpoints). Farmington Hills, MI: Greenhaven Press, 2009.

Fisk, Nathan W. *Understanding Online Piracy: The Truth About Illegal File Sharing*. Santa Barbara, CA: ABC-CLIO, 2009.

Fisk, Nathan, and Marus K. Rogers. *Digital Piracy* (Cybersafety). New York, NY: Chelsea House, 2011.

Hunnewell, Lee. *Internet Piracy*. Edina, MN: ABDO Publishing, 2008.

Johns, Adrian. *Piracy: The Intellectual Property Wars from Gutenberg to Gates*. Chicago, IL: University of Chicago Press, 2010.

Kernfeld, Barry. *Pop Song Piracy: Disobedient Music Distribution Since 1929*. Chicago, IL: University of Chicago Press, 2011.

Mason, Matt. *The Pirate's Dilemma: How Youth Culture Is Reinventing Capitalism*. New York, NY: Free Press, 2009.

Prostigo, Hector. *The Digital Rights Movement: The Role of Technology in Subverting Digital Copyright*. Cambridge, MA: MIT Press, 2012.

Tehranian, John. *Infringement Nation: Copyright 2.0 and You*. New York, NY: Oxford University Press, 2012.

BIBLIOGRAPHY

Bilton, Nick. "Internet Pirates Will Always Win." *New York Times*, August 2012. Retrieved October 2012 (http://www.nytimes.com/2012/08/05/sunday-review/internet-pirates-will-always-win.html?_r=0).

Cambio.com. "Think Twice: Teen Fined $2,900 for Illegally Downloading a Movie." February 24, 2011. Retrieved February 2013 (http://www.cambio.com/2011/02/24/think-twice-teen-fined-2900-for-illegally-downloading-a-movie/).

Dahlstorm, Dana, Daniel Gobrea, Ryan Roemer, and Nabil Schear. *Piracy in the Digital Age*. Berkeley, CA: University of California Press, 2006.

Guertin, Carolyn. *Digital Prohibition: Piracy and Authorship in New Media Art*. New York, NY: Continuum, 2012.

Higgins, George E., and Catherine D. Marcum. *Digital Piracy: An Integrated Theoretical Approach*. Durham, NC: Carolina Academic Press, 2011.

Kusek, David, and Gerd Leonhard. *The Future of Music: Manifesto for the Digital Music Revolution*. Boston, MA: Berklee Press, 2005.

Levine, Robert. *Free Ride: How Digital Parasites Are Destroying the Culture Business, and How the Culture Business Can Fight Back*. New York, NY: Anchor, 2012.

Packard, Ashley. *Digital Media Law*. Malden, MA: Wiley-Blackwell, 2012.

Pfanner, Eric. "Music Industry Counts the Cost of Piracy." *New York Times*, January 21, 2010. Retrieved October 2012 (http://www.nytimes.com/2010/01/22/business/global/22music.html).

Russell, Donnel A., and Trent E. Griffin. *Legislative Approaches to Online Piracy and Copyright Infringement*. New York, NY: Nova Science Publishing, 2012.

Stryszowski, Piotr. *Piracy of Digital Content*. Paris, France: OECD Publishing, 2009.

Torrent Freak.com. "Facebook Uses Torrent, and They Love It." June 25, 2010. Retrieved October 2012 (http://torrentfreak.com/facebook-uses-bittorrent-and-they-love-it-100625).

INDEX

About the Author

Susan Meyer has written a number of titles for Rosen Publishing. She is a big fan of legal digital content and takes full advantage of Netflix for watching far too many movies. Meyer lives and works in Queens, New York.

Photo Credits